DEMOCRACY AND THE PEOPLE

By Tim Damianidis

This eBook was published in 2023 by

M. Damianidis

Fourth Edition

Revision 2

ISBN-13: 978-0-6455221-4-3

For the love of the people.

CONTENTS

Democracy and the people

PROLOGUE

It's never the things that make us happy, that compel us to write, it is the things that have wounded us deeply. This is part of my philosophy for a system known as a Democracy.

1. THE POOR

For a long time, people in a class of poverty have been overlooked by most of the literature available to read. Charles Dickens' Great Expectations was among the few who gave voice to the impoverished. It depicted the difficulty of participation in a system and the forces of the underworld that take children in an undertow.

What would a middle class and beyond know about having to patch torn and worn clothes? What would they know of weaving, sewing or knitting your own clothes? What would the middle class and above know about not affording the books and stationary, that other children have? What would they know of not having shoes to wear? Truancy forced through shame of presenting without uniform or attire or shoes or cleanliness? What would anyone know of sharing a single meal between an entire family? How many of us lit candles or very small fires to keep warm? How many didn't have warm water to bath or shower?

Some argued that communism would give to the poor and take from the rich. But from what we know of communism, under an oligarchy, is that so long as the oligarchy exists, no-one in a commune will be free let alone treated fairly. In fact, the selfishness of the few in power will always outweigh any argument in favour of the poor and needy. Communism controlled by an Oligarchy creates a form of Tyranny.

People opposing communism often thought, perhaps, monetary systems like capitalism could be closer to attaining freedom. But within that system the same type of oligarchy controls the monetary system. Thereby, whoever controls the money controls the system and everyone in it. This becomes apparent in the sense that the mechanisms for self-sufficiency have been controlled to make them not viable. This was done so as to entice people to look for work and jobs. Those that lead at the pyramidal apex, called the Oligarchs, will never let anyone accumulate enough money to achieve anything they don't want. In this way Capitalism controlled by an Oligarchy creates a form of Tyranny.

The poor are known by many names, slaves, workers, servants and so forth. I know the sensitivity of the word slave today implies imperial slavery found throughout the 1700-1800's up until the 21st century. When I speak of slaves I am not speaking of ethnicities or skin colours or any variation of human. When I speak of slave, I speak of what the words imply: doulos from it's Greek origin means servant, worker or someone working for another. The other word, sklavos, from Koine Greek, meaning a captive forced labourer. The later being the type of slaves that were predominantly made of people caught or trapped during the years of the 1700-1800's slave trades. These two words form a very stark extreme view.

Without the chains, whips and mis treatment and without the direct captivity can a person still be a slave? Things change and shift and we can't be stuck with old views that limit how we see things for what they are today and into the future. Nothing takes away the fight of the people who had ancestors trapped and traded like stock. What we add to that is, now they tilted the platform on a different angle but are still playing the same game. You see, what is the difference between a free-range rooster and a caged rooster? They are both captive. Yet one has some choices given to it. One can choose what to eat, the supplied meal or whatever is abundant. The free-range rooster also has the freedom to choose where to move on the property of the owner. Whereas the caged rooster is bound to stay in one place and lacks choices. But at the end, almost all the non-breeding roosters are slaughtered. Are they not enslaved to fulfill one particular function alone? There are some differences but both in my eyes make them strikingly similar to each other. This is how we are in these days. We are given free range without chains and whips, we are given lots of choices but none to be free.

There was never a system in the world that gave a voice to the poor, other than a Democracy. You see a democracy doesn't help you attain wealth or any of those material things, but it gives power to the people. That in it's self empowers the people to make sure they all live well and in good comfort. For a long time the wealthy and powerful along with the middle classes feared losing their possessions. But under the systems of government, we have today, ownership is an illusion. At the end of the day, anything in our hands can be taken by the state under a myriad of laws.

Democracy also required that everyone participated because without participation there can't be a democracy. Democracy isn't for the lazy it's for those that want to participate. In saying that, once people become comfortable they have a tendency to stop participating and from that time onwards, others take over. This contributed to the fate of the Athenian Democracy thousands of years ago, but more importantly it still is the main reason why Democracy often fails today.

2. THE MINORITY DISCRIMINATION

One of the constant problems in any given society is how we treat the minorities. In ancient cities it wasn't so much discrimination but cautious processes of citizenship. This caused most of the situations that may, by our standards, be considered as discrimination. For instance, both parents had to be Athenian citizens and a number of other criteria such as national academy service was needed for a candidate to be considered a citizen. Aristotle said a citizen in paraphrase is someone who has the power to administer the state.

The idea that citizenship should be a reward for having power was not altogether well thought out. This caused many variants in philosophical terms. The survival of the fittest and the rule of the aristoi were two significant developments. What needs to be understood is that when we view the citizen as one as having the power, we also assume they have the ability to hold the power. Thereby, this way of thinking excluded those that are disabled or deliberately kept from having power. In other words, it is a system of aristoi or the most fit to hold power. An elitist view.

A similar system was established by Alexander the Great after he passed away. The generals that took and divided his empire were known as the Diadochi, each waged war against each other, to prove they had the power to possess what they had. So, this ancient view has some merit because, why would you give the best quality paints and utensils to someone who doesn't know how to paint? In the same way why should a citizen be a powerless person? What good will come from such an arrangement? So, we have a dilemma. Yes, being good at something should be rewarded, and if a person can be able to be a citizen they should. But what of the person that lacks the ability or power? What do we do with people who are in a minority that are unable to function as citizens?

Needless to say, that where a person is born is not the issue here. Because many attempts at defining a citizen often led to the idea a person had to be of some place or some lineage or some blood line etc. But in Democratic terms, citizenship is about being able to participate productively in a democratic system. It must be more than a participation but inclusive of a productive manner. Given this, anyone capable can become a citizen. But that is not what is wanted by the system of citizenship. Citizenship is a system to exclude specific minorities from influencing a democratic state or process. Therefore, we can conclude that the only way forward is to create a pathway for non-citizens to become citizens without prejudice or discrimination.

The pathway it's self may be exclusive, for instance, it may exclude one group or another from becoming citizens. In this case the fair thing to do is to also provide these people with a fair way to leave the city or state. The term state used here and throughout means the "kratos"; the holding of power over a region of a city. So, citizenship must be as inclusive as possible but where trust and other matters prevent the society from functioning, there must be a valid and fair way to exit such a system. The founding of a new state elsewhere should not be prohibited provided of course it has the power to withstand antagonism and hostility.

There is ample data around the world that identifies the fact that if you aren't from that place, the chances are you are not going to be treated the same as everyone else. It comes back to our tribal nature. We have clans, tribes, and large families all of which are still existent no matter which system has the holding of power or kratos. This is why minority groups be they religious, cultural, sporting, ideological, behavioral etc. all have some troubles existing and achieving anything of value, to themselves, without being supported externally. This external support is the majority in a Democratic system but could be the Oligarchs or Monarchs in other systems. Usually, the minorities don't get any sympathy or support unless they have a valid issue that could be seen as beneficial to the majority.

Addressing the minority issues by those holding the power has to have a pathway defined that is easy to achieve, practical and possible. Because if the minority are unable to leave the state, then they need a way to be heard and understood and actions need to be taken appropriately. Particular rights and privileges should exist to protect them and make their stay as humane as possible.

3. WELFARE

Where to draw the line has been a growing issue for a long time. For many people who earn some money, they are thrown into a zone called the lower middle class. The lowest class of people happens to be a large number of people with nothing materially, and they suffer significantly in life. The next step up is that of the lower middle class where some income is flowing into the homestead and it can be used to survive in a very minimalistic manner. Usually, these people are able to afford to live under a shelter and provide a meal for their family members. The end result is that the lower middle class usually defines the cut off for welfare. But given today's structure; The lower middle classes are usually trying to pay off debts like those needed to get to work in a motor vehicle. They usually have to pay for medications at full price and yet have nothing left over from their debts to pay for them or even food. Some say they live larger than they should but the essential items such as transport can place people in debt by significant amounts. They take such debts in hope it will assist in getting to their place of work.

The welfare system created by a top down approach, where those at the pinnacle are an Oligarchy, often has trouble fulfilling the role of sincere assistance. To be fair, for example, it should not be an assets based evaluation that determines who receives help. By the asset based evaluation method the gross amounts earned are taken into consideration without truly taking into account expenses. Some would argue this way or that way over these points and even how welfare is distributed. It should be at-least noted that a lot of people on welfare end up better off than some who are working full time. Yet it should also be noted that for whatever reasons some people on welfare can't survive at all and resort to handouts.

In a Democratic system rather than welfare, people were paid to participate in political issues. This meant that people had an income from the state for making and reviewing laws, acting as part of a jury or in the court process and finally to enforce the laws. But the enforcement was usually left to the younger cadets who wanted to become citizens. Career city soldiers, similar to our police, also functioned and trained the cadets. In any case Democracies don't have welfare systems but they cater for everyone by giving them a base retaining income. That income was significant enough to live on comfortably.

4. EDUCATION

An area often left undisturbed is that of institutional education. On one side of things, it is necessary and on the other it guides us away from our own topics of interest. Again, it is a situation of choices given not created by the individual. We are given choices of subjects to study and as we mature these subjects guide us towards a particular way of thinking and writing. By the end of a certain number of years of study, almost everyone will think in a similar manner about a given topic within a school of thought. All the physicists will understand the world in one way that is different to the business and art schools.

Specialisation has taken away generic learning material and replaced it with specific modules of information that teach the population a set and well defined curriculum. The process is to assist in specialising a persons knowledge but in the process it adds blinders to our field of view. While some may know the chemical nature of water, few of those people understand it's spiritual significance.

So, in this way, knowledge is packaged into parts. These parts are also partly true in the sense that the full truth may bridge many disciplines. The full truth is not known by many, in-fact some would argue only God knows the full truth. Yet people strive within their schools of thought to achieve the truth. The same can be said of those in an art chasing it's perfection. After playing guitar since childhood, some people have yet to master it. Despite many hours attempting to, as each day passes there is more to learn from it. When as a person does eventually learn more of the art, age causes the beginning of failing physically from performing. In that the lesson is that the truth about something or its perfection can never truly be achieved. We can approximate the full truth and we can be accurate. However, the complete and full truth or perfection of anything is beyond our human reach. Even those technical components that make up our precision instruments have a leeway of error.

It is therefore important to realise that education is an instrument. It is a tool used to deliver seeds of information and give people inspiration for thought. The same can be said of this attempt to seed the idea that the philosophy of a Democratic state has for a long time been suppressed. That the truth of the Democracy is available to anyone willing to read the works of Plato, Aristotle and numerous others. All I am doing is providing a succinct and concise overview of a subject that deserves your attention.

Who would teach us the one thing that gives us true freedom? If you were in control of a system, would you teach those in it how to control it? If you had all the power in the world, would you use it to give it someone else? Most people would keep power and control over others for as long as they could. You can't blame them for that. But what about yourself and others? Who do you blame for not reading anything to do with the truth? Or perhaps many people are unable to determine what is the truth. Perhaps, those that guide us have guided us to a cliff of devastation. One where everything we know about a democracy has been skewed and twisted to serve a different purpose.

The online dictionaries commonly referred to democracy as a system that allows the election of representatives. A myriad of definitions and defamation exist for the definition. The minute you elect anyone to represent you, is when the power and control have been handed to someone else. Therefore, the word democracy can't apply in this instance. The true meaning of Democracy is, the people's power to operate the state. It must have at it's core the citizens not just deciding but taking roles and duties to keep the system from collapsing. It requires a lot of energy and appetite to remain free.

So then, the first and most important thing to consider is that education of the type that can set us free, is not to be found in specialised books. It is the type of knowledge that has been around for millenniums and exists in philosophies and in literature and all forms of arts and sciences. Yet people need to become teachers themselves. They need to take the role seriously and teach themselves first and then others around them. This is especially true for a subject such as a Democracy. If we do not become teachers of the system, it becomes taught in a skewed manner by others. They falsify and demean the true significant value of it to make it appear like it fails and can't exist. There is a lot to say on the subject but it is worth noting two significant things, without you investigating in the truth, you will never know the truth. The second is that when you investigate the truth be careful of where the knowledge comes from, because if you read some authors, they have alternative motives other than the truth. Aside this book, I recommend the literature of Aristotle, Plato and Socrates. But again, be careful of the translations and who has translated them. Even be cautious of the original fragments, read with caution. If not deliberate, then accidental emotion and skewed biases enter many texts in subtle ways.

In a system of Democracy, education will play a significant role. However, giving the power and control of what is taught to others is a dangerous thing to do. So, then it was up-to teachers to constantly talk and promote Democracy that caused it to change and turn in ancient times. In the same way by talking and discussing it, we learn and progress the philosophical truth of what a Democracy is and how it would operate.

Children with or without the resources to learn from specialised teachers, should have access to learn about the system they intend to control. So, then it would be their guardians who are entrusted with keeping the tradition of the knowledge and teaching it as an obligation or duty.

5. ORDER AND CHAOS

Some would say that freedom is about being able to do anything you want. But what about actions we would not like as a society? Others say that it's about having choices. But who decides on what those choices are? Some argue that no system should be in place and that chaos should rule, in the form of anarchy. But anarchy and chaos have always been associated with each other. How then, could a chaotic state allow for anything but the survival of the fittest and most dominating.

Order then takes away the edge that the most powerful have and puts in place the need for a system that caters for as many as it can. Yes, there will be minorities and people who fall out of the citizenship model. However, the system must be robust enough to ensure that Order is in place through understanding, systematic philanthropy and all manners of ways we can conceive to ensure justice is afforded even to non-citizens or the minority.

Maintaining order is not meant to imply using citizens assigned to the role explicitly but that the system itself has mechanisms to ensure that order is sustained. This means the evasion and treatment of risks that may cause large scale riots, mayhem, chaos and disorder. Mechanisms like ensuring sufficient shelters exist to house the people within the system. Another variable, could be the affordability of life is arranged so that most can attain it. That people's vocations, beliefs and religious callings are all addressed. All these matters are significant to ensuring that order is sustained. These factors alone do not guarantee order but they are some of the variables of concern. Because as highlighted elsewhere, when the people seek immoral and unethical things then the system has failed to create order. Therefore, order is obtainable when there is a balance of ethical needs and the provision of the facilities and infrastructure to achieve those needs. In this way it allows ethical needs not only to be met but also to manifest within the society.

6. DEMOCRACY AND PLEISTOCRACY

One thing people don't realise is that the majority holding the power of the state, doesn't automatically make it a better system. A system of the majority rule is a Pleistocracy and was often given the derogatory term Ochlos or mob rule.

It became clear in the years that followed the Athenian Democracy, circa 450BC, that to distinguish a Democracy from a Pleistocracy meant the quality of the system needed to be evaluated.

The quality of a Democracy was approached by many philosophers and writers in different ways. However, key principles regarding the quality of the Democratic system include;

- a.) The number and proportion of the citizenship participating,
- b.) The time given to the system such as addressing an issue or case,
- c.) The amount, of cases, that require to be addressed in a given time period,
- d.) The size, selection and composition of the juries,
- e.) The process of selection by lot over election,
- f.) Randomisation incorporated within the system,
- g.) Experience preserved in short term, rotating and altering positions of prominence, such as Archons,

15

h.) Ethics and values held by the majority.

Ultimately, when the people have the power to write their laws, judge themselves and enforce those laws themselves, then we have the core components to a democratic state. That is to say that the three main areas of a Democratic system are that the people hold power over the:

a.) Legislature,

b.) Judiciary,

c.) and Enforcement.

But two things stand out more than anything else. There has to be respect for each other and there needs to be a set of common ethics. There has to be a set of ethics that people must abide by. These ethics form the most fundamentally challenging and most critical points upon which the whole system is based.

You see, in a system that's not a Democracy, the ethics of the people and what they consider as ethical and valued are distorted by those that control them. This creates an apostacy of political views and distorts the fundamental reality of the people. By dividing people into small niche groups and many of them, they are able to control multiple minority groups. This is how the religious understand the division of the Christian church. Satanic influences divided Christians into numerous groups and what they called heretical worship before the Great Schism. Then the entity, called the Church, became a myriad of denominations since then. Over 40,000 minority groups all controlled and channelled by those that form the Oligarchy. To be clear the Oligarchs are those that have the power to control governments and nations.

So, if it is not a Christian Democracy, what would it be? I can't see any other religion working hand in hand with a Democratic state. The content of it lends to it's valuable use within a Democratic system. It's values and ethics are what will help distinguish a Democracy from a Pleistocracy.

7. DEMOCRACY

The model of a democracy is based on the people empowering themselves. It can not be a case of others giving the people power. Therefore, the only way that a Democracy can function is when the people are united and at-least form a movement encompassing the majority.

There are many more factors to consider as already stated, the quality of the people will determine if that majority is ethical or some kind of mob. It is devastatingly fearsome to be judge by imbeciles and thugs. This is why ethics and values are so important to communicate and instil in a society. Without the proper ethics and values a Democracy just can't function. It is no surprise that the people have become corrupted by immorality. Yes, there has always been some immorality but the extent to which it occurs world wide is unparalleled aside the, biblically mentioned, historic cities of Sodom and Gamora.

Immorality creates the type of chaos that prevents unity. All forms of somatic based corruption exist be it sexual, drug related, addictions and perversions and so much more to do with the body. It is the somatic based corruptions that create violence and other actions normally unseen in a society. Therefore, it is imperative that the focus of the people, should be to focus on themselves and ensure that they themselves are as ethical as possible.

Having established the three main parts of the Democratic system, it is important to provide further details as to it's composition. What follows is a descriptive of a democratic system based on that written by Aristotle. However, to make it modern in terminology I have not used the same vocabulary nor is the system described exactly as is mentioned by Aristotle. It is merely based on that system and does not actually exist in the world at the time of writing this.

The church

The church, ecclesia or popular assembly or general assembly all refer to the same main part of the system. It is the people gathered for the purpose of making decisions. The people are the central part of the entire system and form the most populous component. Each city district was given participation rights. So if a city's regions are divided into 12 parts each of those 12 areas would have a group of people not representing but participating in government. It was varied in composition in history, sometimes it was small in numbers and could have been mistaken for a meeting place for each of the tribes of Athens. At others it may have seemed extremely overly populous.

The council

The people require specialised services in terms of administration, supervisors, law writers and other people that can perform a technical duty to assist when asked to assist. This part was known as the Boule. It is the council that takes orders from the people. The council in return drafts laws, administers the process of the Assembly and deals with disputes.

The Tribunal

Then after these things are established the next civilian entity is that of the Popular Tribunal. This again is made up of short term workers with specialised skills. This can be seen as temporary Law reviewers and writers who may send back a law to the people with comments. It would include judges with specialised skills in civil and criminal matters, it would also include supervisors, auditors and inspectors checking on those within this part of the system.

The Aeropagus

The supreme court was called the Ancient Tribunal (Aeropagus) and was comprised of judges whom oversaw serious cases such as homicide. These judges rotated in activity but remained in a pool known as retired Archons.

Military Magistrates

The other areas of policing the system and it's military defence were left to those with the ability to do so. However, as with all other instances, a position was always filled by the drawing of lots. Elections were never used unless it was among those seeking technical assistants and other non-systemic positions. The people could elect at any time a person to take a position of technical nature but not ever within the system. For example, there may only be a few people who know how to build ships and these people would be put into a pool of whom could be elected to perform a duty for the military. But once that duty was fulfilled their service expired.

The Archons

Civil magistrates were usually people who had skills in areas of law, enforcement and legislature. They also had contributed to society in such a way that they were considered Archons or leaders. Again, all vacancies for active positions were selected by lot not vote. There were several positions like a family name celebrant, a military leader, a prestigious person and citizens representing each tribe or district. These were the Archons and civil magistrates.

We could elaborate further on this system but what is described so far forms the basis of how a democracy could be implemented. There are Five auxiliary parts with the Sixth being the central Assembly of the people and the Seventh being the citizen population including those that don't participate.

Key elements to remember are that the tribes require equal representation in every part of the system. So the minimum number of people in this system, using 12 tribes as an example, is 12 participants x 6 parts = 72. In some cases, each of the tribes may want an Archon for their military meaning there would be 12 for each position held. This inflates the numbers involved but ensures fair distribution of power.

It was also typical that each month of the year saw a different tribe lead the Democracy, meaning that the tribe participants were eligible to organise the affairs of the system as long as they didn't change the system. If the decisions of the month were considered biased or impacted one tribe over another it could be reversed or changed the next month.

ABOUT THE AUTHOR

Tim Damianidis is a business person and family man with connections around the world. He has a Graduate Diploma in Occupational Health and Safety and has worked in numerous businesses.